I0488232

Survival Family Basics
The Death of Money

*The Prepper's Guide to
Economic Collapse, the
Loss of Paper Wealth, and
What to Do When Money
Dies*

Macenzie Guiver

© 2014

All Rights Reserved. **No part of this publication may be reproduced in any form or by any means, including scanning, photocopying, or otherwise without prior written permission of the copyright holder.**

Disclaimer and Terms of Use: The Author and Publisher have strived to be as accurate and complete as possible in the creation of this book, notwithstanding the fact that he does not warrant or represent at any time that the contents within are accurate due to the rapidly changing nature of the Internet. While all attempts have been made to verify information provided in this publication, the Author and Publisher assume no responsibility for errors, omissions, or contrary interpretation of the subject matter herein. Any perceived slights of specific persons, peoples, or organizations are unintentional. In practical advice books, like anything else in life, there are no guarantees of income made or health benefits received. This book is not intended for use as a source of medical, legal, business, accounting or financial advice. All readers are advised to seek services of competent professionals in medical, legal, business, accounting, and finance matters.

Printed in the United States of America

Just to say Thank You for Purchasing this Book
I want to give you a gift 100% absolutely FREE

A Copy of My Upcoming Special Report "The
Prepper's Supplies Guide for When Disaster
Strikes"

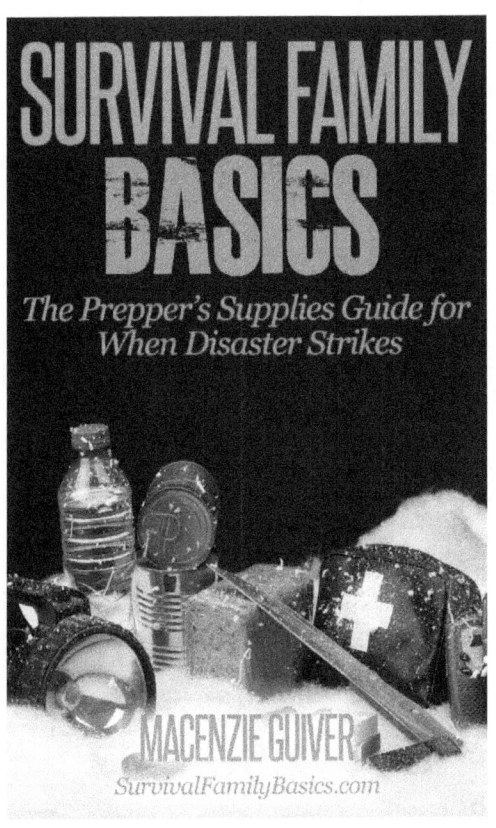

Go to <u>www.SurvivalFamilyBasics.com</u> to Sign
Up to Receive Your FREE Gift

Table of Contents

Introduction

I want to thank you and congratulate you for purchasing, *"The Death of Money: The Prepper's Guide to Economic Collapse, the Loss of Paper Wealth, and What to Do When Money Dies"*.

It is difficult for many people to wrap their heads around the idea that our economy, the biggest in the world, could somehow collapse or that our currency, which other countries turn to in times of turmoil, might crash. Unfortunately it's not only possible, it came close to happening in the fall of 2008, and the danger has only increased since then.

Much of the discussion around economic collapse centers on mistrust of the government and the national debt, but these are not the only potential problems that plague our nation's economy. Rather than focus on the politics or the people, this guide dives into the sources of economic strife in order to provide an in-depth understanding of what an economic collapse would mean for you and your family.

This guide will introduce you to the possible causes of an economic collapse and outline the kinds of impacts you can expect for each. It will walk you through the five stages of collapse and show you what you can do from a preparedness perspective to be ready to weather each stage.

We'll wrap up with some actionable steps that you can take right now to position your family to survive and thrive during difficult economic times.

From explaining what causes hyperinflation to outlining what happens when the government can't pay its bills, this guide gives you the information you need to understand the potential causes of economic crisis, strengthen your family's position *now* in preparation for dire economic conditions, and assemble the skills and supplies you will need to safeguard your family's future if the economy turns upside down.

Thanks again for purchasing this book. I hope you enjoy it!

Macenzie Guiver

How Money Might Die

When we talk about the death of money what we really mean is some kind of catastrophic economic collapse, which in and of itself, defies easy definition. The term economic collapse can be used to describe a broad range of scenarios that each carries a different set of consequences and possible ramifications for the way we live our lives. This is one of the reasons many people fail to adequately prepare for this kind of scenario. The ambiguous nature of the threat can make it difficult to get your head around. Unlike a natural disaster like a hurricane or an earthquake, the steps to preparedness are less clear and more open to individual interpretation.

Regardless of the challenge prepping for an economic collapse presents, the potential impact to society as a whole is so great that it must be one of the scenarios every family that is serious about prepping must consider. In an attempt to break the issue down and help you identify the steps you and your family need to take in order to be ready for this kind of disaster, let's start by looking at what conditions are commonly included under the "economic collapse" umbrella.

This term has been used to describe several different economic conditions. These conditions range from prolonged depression like the one the U.S. experienced in the 1930's to hyperinflation and high unemployment. As history has shown us, when societies experience tumultuous economic conditions these conditions are often accompanied by social upheaval, civil unrest, and the loss of the rule of law.

Economic collapse and the conditions associated with it are rarely caused by a single event or decision. This is one of the reasons they can be so difficult to nail down and even more difficult to anticipate or plan for. In order to effectively prep for anything, you need to first understand the nature of that threat. So, to start, let's explore the different economic challenges that we need to be prepared to withstand.

Possible Causes

Hyperinflation

Hyperinflation is the term used to describe a sudden and rapid increase in the price of consumer goods and the corresponding devaluation of currency. Hyperinflation almost always occurs when a government that has been operating with a huge budget deficit attempts to finance that debt by creating more money. As this new money begins to flood the market, the overall value of that currency degrades meaning consumers need to spend more to get the same thing. The rapid increase in prices creates consumer panic and mistrust of the government issued currency. When this happens, people immediately begin buying whatever *real* goods (as opposed to paper notes) are available in an effort to safeguard their wealth. This creates a rapidly escalating cycle where increased demand causes prices to soar while mistrust of the local currency causes rapid devaluation as people dump currency in favor of real goods that will retain their value.

In essence, hyperinflation occurs when people no longer believe that the money in their pocket will be as valuable tomorrow as it is today so they spend it on something they feel will continue to be as valuable tomorrow as it is right now.

Hyperinflation is commonly seen in the aftermath of war, social upheaval, natural disaster, and other unrelated crises that impact a country's ability to collect taxes or borrow money which forces them to use money creation for financing.

From a preparedness perspective, the immediate implications of hyperinflation are:

- Skyrocketing prices of essential goods
- Bank runs
- Contraction of the credit market
- Rapid decreases in buying power
- Rapid devaluation of the local currency
- Adoption of a foreign currency as standard
- Rapid divestiture of local currency in favor of goods that will better retain their value
- Return of a barter based economy

Historically, the only way to end hyperinflation is through aggressive policy changes unless the root cause of the hyperinflation is civil war. Hyperinflation resulting from civil war often ends once the war ends and one side wins.

Examples

- Hungary 1946 – Prices were doubling every 15 hours and the inflation rate was 13, 600, 000, 000, 000, 000% per month.
- Zimbabwe 2008 – Prices doubled about every 24 hours and the inflation rate exceeded 75,000,000,000%. A loaf of bread cost $35 million.
- Yugoslavia 1994 – Prices doubled every 34 hours and the inflation rate rose by 313,000,000% in a single month.
- Weimar Germany 1923 – Prices doubled every 3 ½ days and the rate of inflation was 29,500% and the price of a pound of bread was $3 billion.

Deflation

For all intents and purposes, deflation is the opposite of hyperinflation. The value of currency increases as the price of goods and services falls. While that might sound like a good scenario, it can have catastrophic consequences, especially if it devolves into a deflationary spiral. During deflation, the supply of money decreases at the same time that the supply of goods increases. People hoard currency instead of real goods because they believe the currency will be worth more tomorrow than it is today. When demand decreases, prices fall taking wages and income with them. People buy less so companies produce less which means people make less and the cycle repeats. As the spiral continues downward price points become unprofitable, businesses fail, job losses mount, and unemployment soars.

Unlike some of the other economic conditions outlined here, deflation is not generally something that happens rapidly or that requires an immediate preparedness response.

From a preparedness perspective, the long term implications of deflation are:

- Loss of jobs and increased unemployment
- Economic depression
- The value of debt increases
- Banks and businesses fail
- Credit becomes difficult to obtain
- Investment decreases
- People begin hoarding money instead of goods
- Civil unrest

Examples

The most relatable example of deflation for most preppers is the Great Depression. While deflation was not the sole cause of the depression, it was a big contributing factor. Since most people are very familiar with the Great Depression and its effects on society, I am not going to go into detail here. You can find an overview of this time in our history here (http://en.wikipedia.org/wiki/Great_Depression).

Major Market Crash

Major markets like the stock market, bond market, and markets for commodities like corn or silver are prone to cycles of boom and bust. We don't need to look back too far in history to see what can happen when there is a sudden decline in the price of a specific commodity or across a section of the market. Market crashes are volatile and while they are related to the economic conditions of the time, there are other factors at play that can cause market crashes that defy expectations.

Panic and speculation are key components of a market crash and play a much bigger role here than they do in the other possible causes of collapse. While economic events or conditions are at the heart of any market crash, there is a social element and a mob mentality that isn't normally seen at the beginning of other collapse conditions. Where the psychology of the crowd plays a big role during the peak of other events like hyperinflation, an economic depression, or a natural disaster, it is rarely the cause of the collapse. But in a market collapse, this kind of group-think hysteria can actually be the trigger for the entire event.

During a market crash, there is a sudden sell-off by one or more participants of a specific commodity, stock, or option that becomes contagious and spreads rapidly across the market. Once the selling starts, the price of that stock or commodity will begin to drop which encourages other sellers to sell as well in an effort to get out before the asset loses all of its value. When this happens to a single asset, it is called a sell-off but it can easily spread across an entire section of the market or to the entire market as a whole causing a massive divestiture.

From a preparedness perspective, the immediate implications of a market crash are:

- Loss of wealth
- Economic depression
- Failure of banks and businesses
- Loss of confidence in the market
- Loss of confidence in the economy
- People stop spending which creates the conditions for deflation

Examples

- October 29, 1929 - The Great Crash aka Black Tuesday remains the most devastating stock market crash in the history of the U.S. The Dow Jones Industrial Average lost 90% of its value as a result of this crash and it would be 25 years before it would rise to its pre-crash peak. It signified the start of the Great Depression that would last for 10 years and reduced millionaires to paupers overnight.

- March 27, 1980 - Silver Thursday or the crash of the U.S. silver commodity markets resulting from the implementation of Silver Rule 7 which restricted the use of leveraging and caused silver prices to fall by 50% in 4 days.

- October 19, 1987 – Black Monday stock markets around the world crashed, beginning with the Hong Kong market and following the sun to spread through Europe and into the U.S.. The Dow Jones Industrial Average (DJIA) dropped by 508 points in a single day losing more than 22% of its value which remains the biggest single day drop in history.

- October 13, 1989 - Friday the 13th Mini-Crash occurred when a failed leverage buyout of the UAL Corporation, parent company of United Airlines triggered the collapse of the junk bond market. The DJIA lost 190.58 points and 6.9% of its value with the transportation sector falling by more than 12%.

- October 27, 1997 - Global stock market crash resulting from an economic crisis in Asia. The Dow Jones Industrial Average suffered its eighth largest point loss in in history.

- September 16, 2008 – Subprime Mortgage Crisis begins and rapidly evolves into a global financial crisis that continues today, the ramifications of which are not yet known. Although it is not the same kind of "crash" as others on this list, the catastrophic effect on the U.S. housing market alone is reason enough to include it here.

- May 6, 2010 - Flash Crash occurs when the Dow Jones Industrial Average drops almost 1000 points but recovers those losses in minutes. It is the single biggest intraday drop in the history of the DJIA.

Catastrophe or Disaster

Natural and man-made disasters can have significant and immediate economic consequences on regions and entire countries. This impact starts with the real dollar losses associated with the kinds of physical damage that can be caused by hurricanes, tornados, earthquakes, tsunamis, and other disasters. In Hurricane Katrina alone, physical damage was estimated at over $100 billion dollars. But the economic impact doesn't end with the actual damage. Natural and man-made disasters also result in wide spread relocation, unemployment, loss of revenue, loss of business opportunity, and loss of businesses. Depending on the location of the disaster and the resulting damage, disruptions in the movement of goods and services to unaffected areas can also occur causing additional economic impacts.

From a preparedness perspective, the immediate implications of a natural disaster or catastrophe are likely the most well known across the prepping community. As this is an area where most prepping families already devote much of their time, I won't be discussing it further. The important thing to note is that a natural or man-made disaster can be the triggering event for an economic collapse.

The Stages of Economic Collapse

Looking across history, we can see that when economic collapse happens it follows a standard pattern flowing through a series of stages. While these stages do not always happen in a linear fashion or even one at a time, it is important to understand the kinds of impacts you can expect as the different parts of our society falter, founder, and fall.

Stage 1: The Decay of Our Financial Foundations

Stage 1 is the decay of the financial foundation upon which the economy is built. It begins with the loss of faith in financial markets and represents the beginning of the end of business as usual. Income inequality, financial insecurity, and the perceived instability combine to create a distrust of markets, financial institutions, politicians, and economic forecasts. This stage is signified by an unwillingness to take financial risks caused by a lack of belief in a better financial future. It can be designated by the failure of financial institutions, the loss of savings and accumulated wealth, and the inaccessibility of capital for investment or lending.

Many people believe we have already passed through this stage while others believe this is where our economy currently stands.

This stage of economic collapse can cause:

- People to lose their homes or be forced to move to other cities to find work or because housing has become unaffordable
- Decreases in wages
- Decreases in median household income
- Overvalued asset bubbles to burst
- Wealth to decrease

- Credit policies to constrict
- Unemployment
- Currency devaluation

At this stage, the primary economic assets you need to have in place to survive and thrive are a career with a steady paycheck, a house with some equity, money in a savings account, investments in stocks, bonds, and retirement accounts, health insurance, and a good credit rating. As long as you have the majority of these economic assets, you will be able to weather this stage of economic collapse without much difficulty.

Stage 2: The Contraction of Commerce

Stage 2 is the contraction of the day to day commerce that underpins our capitalist society. It begins with a rapid decline in consumer confidence spurred by high unemployment, sluggish growth, and further loss of faith in the financial and social safeguards we used to take for granted. More and more people require government assistance just to survive and even working families struggle to put food on the table. The government must borrow more and more money simply to provide essential services to those who are unable to support themselves because of widespread job losses and increasing rates of unemployment.

As people make less money and feel less secure about their financial future, they change their spending habits, holding on to their money longer and foregoing the purchase of everything from luxury items like new cars and family vacations to necessities like heating oil and medical care. Discretionary income is used to purchase things like gold, silver, alcohol, medical supplies, fuel, and other supplies that are more likely to retain their value over time. Increased demand for these items drives sends prices soaring.

At the same time, less spending and less income means less tax revenue. The already overextended government is forced to continue to borrow money simply to finance the rapidly expanding debt and maintain essential services.... until the day that it can't. The day comes when our collective creditors decide we have become a bad credit risk and refuse to extend any more credit.

Unable to borrow money, the government will have only two choices.

1. Make drastic cuts across all areas of the federal government resulting in massive layoffs of government workers, the suspension of all non-debt related payments including social security, welfare, medicare, and federal/military pensions, and the recall of all military personnel from abroad.

2. Start printing money in order to be able to make debt payments and continue operating with only essential personnel, similar to what happens during a government shutdown.

The ripple effects of either of these options can be catastrophic ranging from hyperinflation to armed revolt. The flow of goods across the country will be disrupted along with international trade. People will be standing in food lines as store shelves stand empty and banks will be forced to close to remain closed to avoid massive withdrawals that would further destabilize the economy.

Many people feel we are in the early part of this stage now.

This stage of economic collapse can cause:

- Hyperinflation
- Hoarding
- Price gouging
- Significant increases in unemployment
- Scarcity of goods
- Credit to become unavailable
- The breakdown of the social safety net
- Food riots
- Civil unrest

At this stage, the primary economic assets you need to have in place to survive and thrive are a job that remains stable despite increasing instability and skills that you can parlay into another job or freelancing should your seemingly stable job "disappear", a stockpile of gold, silver, and precious metals, cash on hand, a home with equity, health insurance, and no debt. As long as you have the majority of these economic assets, you will have what you need to take care of your family through this stage of the collapse.

Stage 3: The Rise of Revolution

Stage 3 is the point at which every day Americans stop waiting for someone to save them and realize their fate is in their own hands. It begins once people comprehend the dire nature of our new circumstances. The government implements a variety of economic policies in an effort to stabilize the collapsing economy to no avail. Unemployment continues to rise and more and more middle class families find themselves homeless, out of money, and unable to obtain the basic necessities of life like food, clean water, and basic medical care. Rampant printing of money by the government in an attempt to keep creditors at bay has devalued the dollar to such a degree that currencies all over the world are devolving as their U.S. dollar backed economies crash and burn.

Hyperinflation sets in and regular Americans are rioting in the streets demanding food, services, and answers. A failed attempt to confiscate the firearms of law abiding citizens results in violent confrontations that pit American soldiers against American citizens. Martial law is imposed, movement, speech, and congregation are restricted and angry citizens begin talking about open revolt.

This stage of economic collapse can cause:

- Hyperinflation
- Hoarding
- Scarcity of goods
- Food riots
- Civil unrest
- Violent confrontations
- Global economic collapse
- The loss of basic freedoms
- Development of a black market barter based economy

At this stage, the primary economic assets you need to have in place to survive and thrive are a stockpile of gold, silver, precious metals and other goods that can be bartered, a home stocked with food, water, medicine, and fuel, firearms, ammunition, and the skills required to defend and take care of your family. The world will be a much more dangerous place and you and your family members will need to adjust everything about how you live, what you think, and who you trust in order to get by. Having these assets on hand will ensure you have access to the resources you need to care for your family without having to rely on external sources.

Stage 4: The Cessation of Society

Stage 4 is the end of society as we know it. It begins when essential services become unreliable and unobtainable and people desperate for food and safety find only martial law and draconian ruthlessness when they look to their government. Hyperinflation continues and members of the armed forces leave their posts to look after their families when month after month passes without pay. Armed militias form, staking claim to neighborhoods and rural areas. Violent skirmishes are common as people fight for limited resources.

The power grid becomes unstable and entire neighborhoods of houses sit empty and abandoned. Skills like farming, gardening, raising livestock, food production, first aid, and medical care are the most valuable commodities. People without the skills to take care of their families begin to starve and die of treatable medical problems in large numbers. Basic utilities like electricity and running water fail everywhere as the violence escalates and survival becomes your only concern.

This stage of economic collapse can cause:

- Currency collapse
- Loss of essential services
- Famine
- Rapidly increasing death rate
- Open revolt
- Wide spread violence
- Societal collapse

- The end of the rule of law
- Rampant instances of rape, murder, abduction, slavery

At this stage, the primary economic assets you need to have in place to survive and thrive are a defensible rural home stocked with food, water, medicine, and fuel for long term survival, firearms, ammunition, and the skills required to defend and take care of your family completely on your own. This is Syria. This is the Wild West. This is life like it was in the 1700 and 1800's. Those without the skills to survive on their own will be easy prey for those who are stronger and better armed. You will need the will and the skill to defend what's yours and provide everything needed to survive. Having these assets on hand gives you the best chance at surviving in an increasingly hostile and dangerous world.

Stage 5: The Collapse of Our Culture

Stage 5 is the point at which our culture is crushed under the weight of a collapsing society. It begins when someone amasses enough people and resources to seize power and install themselves and their followers as a totalitarian regime. The size of the country means it is unlikely that any one faction will be able to exert enough control to seize control of more than a region or a state. This means small nation states or city states will pop up like the Free State of New York City and the Northern Alliance which encompasses most of the New England states. Ideas like freedom, liberty, independence, voting, and rights will be sacrificed for safety, security, and survival. Nation states will fight each other for resources while also fighting whatever remains of the federal government for control of the assets, resources, and people within their self-proclaimed boundaries.

The people within these nation states will have little choice but to align with the new regime or flee to another district. The laws, rights, and allocation of resources will differ from nation state to nation state and those who find themselves in the minority will be subject to persecution and other social injustices. The citizens of the former United States of America will finally understand why it was so important to intervene on behalf of the citizens of other countries who were being persecuted and murdered by their own governments. Unfortunately, there won't be anyone to swoop in and save us because much of the rest of the world will be dealing with collapses and crashes of their own.

This stage of economic collapse can cause:

- Third world conditions
- The rise of warlords
- Famine and starvation
- Disease
- Wide spread violence
- Loss of all basic rights and freedoms
- State sanctioned rape, murder, abduction, slavery
- Persecution

At this stage, in all honesty, you need to hope that you are aligned with whatever group rises up to seize control of the region you inhabit. Or, plan to be far enough away from civilization that no one knows or cares you are there. This will look like the dystopian worlds portrayed in every bad post-apocalyptic movie. Your only chance at survival is to be resourceful and skilled enough to either make it on your own or to carve out some niche in the new world order that will allow you to protect and provide for your family.

Living in a World without Money

For many of us, the idea of existing in a world without money is simply unfathomable. And yet, an economy based around a state-backed currency tied to nothing is something that would have seemed equally foreign and outlandish to our great-great grandparents. As recently as the early 1800's there was no national currency and people used barter and precious metals to get what they needed.

While the concept of currency (something used as a medium of exchange) has been around since 3000 BCE in Mesopotamia, and coins were first minted in the East in 11th century BCE China and 6th century BCE Greece and Rome, currencies have almost always been backed by something of value. In fact in the U.S. up until 1962 paper money was "Payable to the Bearer on Demand," meaning you could exchange your paper notes for the gold or silver that they represented.

In 1944 when most of the world was suffering from the economic ravages of still-raging World War II the U.S. dollar was made the reserve currency of the world (meaning exchanges of money between countries had to be conducted in U.S. dollars). Ours was the most stable currency and backed by our significant gold reserves, so the plan made sense at the time. In 1971, however, when President Nixon took the U.S. off the gold standard the the entire world began operating on a completely fiat currency system (meaning using money that is backed by nothing other than the government's say-so – no gold, no silver, just paper and a promise). Never in the history of the world has a fiat currency *NOT* crashed, and the average life expectancy of one is 27 years. You can do the math on that one. And never in the history of the world has the *entire* world been using them all at the same time.

In some ways, I think the internet generation may be even worse off than our parents and grandparents will be when a crash comes. This is because most of us find the use of physical money quite antiquated, preferring to keep all our financial transactions in the virtual world. This means that we will already be behind the game when cash, precious metals, or things of *real* tangible value become king because we never use physical money, just transact in computer conversions behind the scenes. Even more importantly, we aren't likely to have anything of value stored in the real world which leaves us incredibly exposed to any disruption in the virtual economy.

So the good news is, living in a world without money as we understand it today is something humans have done for most of our history. The bad news is…. we don't really know how to do it anymore and are completely unprepared for it.

In fact, the majority of us lack the skills required to produce the goods and provide the services that will enable us to barter for what we will need. You might be making bank right now writing computer code but that isn't going to help you when the power goes out and the only way your family will eat today is if you can find something to eat, kill something to eat, or trade for something to eat.

So, what can you do right now to make sure your family can weather whatever economic storm comes our way and survive if the worst happens and the bottom drops out of the dollar? The same things you need to do to prepare for other potential catastrophes – strengthen your position, build your skills, and stockpile supplies.

Strengthen Your Position

The economy doesn't have to collapse to have a significant impact on your family. Anyone who has lived through the last 7 years can testify to that, which is why the first thing you need to do is strengthen your overall position. This means making smart decisions about your own finances that will position you to survive and thrive through the different stages of economic collapse. Here are my best tips for strengthening your overall economic and financial position.

- Keep your money close and do whatever you can to pay off any debt beyond your home.
- Pay down the mortgage on your home when you can, but focus on other debt first.
- Avoid the stock market.
- Don't keep all your money in one bank.
- Don't keep all your money in the bank.
- Make sure you have enough low-denomination cash on hand to meet your family's basic needs for at least 2-4 weeks. (This means buying things not paying bills).
- Save up until you have an emergency fund that will allow you to pay any non-discretionary bills for 6 months. (cable is discretionary, the mortgage is not)
- Put some of your money into small pieces of precious metals like silver and gold but don't go overboard. Useable goods will always be tradable items but starving people may be unwilling to trade for a piece of metal, no matter how much it is worth.

The lists provided in the following sections were compiled from my own knowledge of prepping for long term disasters and from reviewing accounts of survivors of economic collapse, civil war, and other catastrophic conditions. As always, the first focus must be on building skills before moving on to stockpiling supplies.

Skills to Build

- Bartering
- Hunting
- Fishing
- Butchering
- Raising Livestock
- Gardening
- Mining
- Construction
- Engineering
- First Aid and Emergency Medicine
- Food Production (Cheese, Butter, Bread)
- Marksmanship
- Making Ammo
- Pottery
- Carving and Whittling
- Sewing, Knitting, and Crochet
- Making and Administering Herbal Remedies
- Water Purification
- Fire Making and Tending
- Beer and Wine Making
- Cooking Using Unconventional Means
- Candle Making

Things to Stockpile

- Water and Water Purification Supplies – Without clean water, you can survive for 3 to 5 days. Drinking contaminated water can kill you in less than a day. To say that providing the means to maintain a safe supply of potable water is the most important thing you can do is an understatement. It won't matter how many guns you own or how many boxes of ammo are under your bed if you die of dysentery from drinking dirty water.

- Food – Make sure you have enough food stored to meet the needs of your family for at least 6 months at 150%. This means that a family of 6 will need enough food for 9 people. Don't forget to stockpile things like salt, sugar, honey, tea, coffee, and spices. If you have infants or are of child-bearing age make sure to include formula. Make sure canned gravy is on your list as it can be used to make dry, gamey, unappetizing meat and other food more palatable.

- Fire Starters – Anything that can be used to make fire including matches, magnesium fire starters, flint and steel.

- Medical Supplies – Antibiotics, antibiotic cream, anti-diarrheal medication, fever reducers, bandages, and latex gloves can mean the difference between life and death for the members of your family in a world without access to essential services like running water and medical care. Don't forget to stockpile prescription medications, especially those that are used to manage life-threatening chronic medical conditions.

- Fuel - This is an absolute essential most people fail to adequately stockpile. Worry less about how you are going to fuel your car and more about how you will keep your family warm when it comes to determining the type(s) and amount of fuel to stockpile. Don't forget to include lamp oil and if using fire for cooking or heating is a part of your plan, you will need to stockpile seasoned hardwood.

- Hygiene Supplies – In a world without basic services cleanliness is more important than godliness and you need to have things like soap, bleach, toilet paper, toothpaste, floss, garbage bags, Kleenex, and cloth diapers on hand that will help safeguard the health of your family. You should also stockpile condoms because the last thing anyone needs in the apocalypse is an unplanned pregnancy.

- Seeds – Seeds give you options as they can be used to produce food, they can be used to grow herbs and spices, and they can be used for barter. If you plan to stockpile seeds you will also need to develop the skills required to do something with them unless your only purpose is to use them to barter for the things you need.

- Ammunition – It won't do you much good to stockpile all these supplies if you have no way of defending your stockpile from someone who wants to come and take it.

- Knives – There was a time when everyone walked around with a knife on their belt because it was a necessary tool for everyday living. Today, most people don't even carry a pocket knife. Make it a priority to purchase several high quality knives for the members of your family and the tools you will need to sharpen them.

- Vinegar and baking soda – These two items are often left off of many prepping "must have" lists which I think is a crime. They can be used for everything from killing weeds to cleaning your house to cooking your food. A stockpile of both is an absolute essential.

- Hand tools – Stockpiling small non-electric hand tools like axes, hatchets, saws, screwdrivers, hammers, hand pumps, and siphons will ensure you have these things available for your own use in building and repairing things, and that you will have them to use in bartering. Don't forget to include something to use to sharpen blades.

- Aluminum foil, duct tape, and paracord – These items will be worth their weight in gold to you and those you trade with because they are incredibly useful, especially in a post-collapse world.

- Fishing supplies – Being able to source food from local lakes and rivers requires these supplies and basic fishing skills. Remember, in many scenarios, your family's survival will depend on your ability to procure enough food to meet their nutritional needs. Fishing is ideal because it requires less skill and energy than hunting.

- Resource and Reference Books – Build a library of resource and reference books that will help you learn to do the things you don't have the time or the energy to learn to do right now. Don't rely on the .pdfs you have on your iPad or the vast information accessible via Google because there is no guarantee you will have electricity or a computer to access them.

- Sewing, Knitting, and Crocheting Supplies – Another area I often see overlooked on lists of important prepping supplies for long term survival are the supplies needed to mend and make clothing and other items. The lives we live today are much less active than the lives we will have to live post-collapse and a more active lifestyle means you will be much harder on your clothes. Mending will become an important task since the supply of post-collapse clothing will quickly be claimed.

- Pest Control Supplies – One of the most common items found on lists created by disaster survivors are ant traps, mouse traps, rat poison, and roach traps as war, unrest, poor sanitation, and unhygienic conditions are breeding grounds for these pests. Because they can spread disease and compromise your food supply, it is a good idea to stockpile supplies for controlling any infestation, even if you don't have any problems with these pests now.

- Luxury Items – Keeping morale up is important when the world seems to be falling apart around you and simple, small luxuries like a piece of chocolate, a bottle of hand lotion, a deck of cards, a novel, or a cup of hot chocolate can work miracles in desperate times. These items are also excellent for barter.

Other Items Worth Investing In Now

While these items are important, they aren't necessarily the kind of thing you would want to stockpile.

- Solar Generator
- Portable Shower
- Oil Lamps
- Firearms
- Cast Iron Cookware

- Hand-operated appliances like a can opener, hand mixer, grain mill, coffee grinder, etc.
- Laundry tub, clothes wringer, clothesline
- Gas grill, cook stove, or other alternative option for cooking
- Warm woolen clothing, extra gloves, winter outerwear, long underwear, extra socks, rain gear, rain boots, work gloves, and sturdy boots for all family members
- Fire extinguishers for every room
- Bicycles
- Camping equipment including tents, sleeping bags, lanterns, a cookstove, a cooler, etc.
- Hand pump for a well

Bartering Basics

There is no reason you can't start honing your bartering skills now so that you have a leg up during and after an economic collapse. The easiest way to get started is to go to Craigslist and offer something you have but no longer want up for trade. Once you have a potential trading partner, you can start working on your bartering skills with these tips.

1. Know What it's Worth… to You
The first step to bartering successfully is to know what the item you are looking to trade is worth. This can mean market value but it can also mean what it is worth to you. For example, I inherited an ugly boat a few years ago that was just sitting in my driveway. I am fairly certain that the boat itself was worth about $500 if I wanted to take the time and expend the energy to sell it. But what I really wanted was to get it out of my yard. I decided that the minimum I would take for it was a trade worth about $50.

This is an important point because bartering is all about getting what you want or what you need. I needed to get that ugly boat out of my driveway and I didn't want to have to do it myself. To me, trading for some lilac bushes and two apple trees, which would have cost me more than $50 at the local nursery, was a solid trade even though it didn't approach my assumed market value.

2. Be Ready to Walk Away

Not every potential trading partner is going to be a peach. Odds are, most of the offers you get will be low-ball offers that don't meet your needs. Don't feel obligated to accept an offer that doesn't suit you.

3. Focus on Trading Fairly instead of Trading Up

There is a lot of focus in the bartering world on trying to trade up anytime you make a trade. I blame reality TV and the Barter Kings for instilling the idea that every trade should be getting you something worth more than what you are giving. To me, that feels dishonest and as if you are trying to swindle people. In today's world that may be a little unethical by some people's standards. But in a world of economic turmoil and societal collapse, that kind of thinking can get you killed.

I don't mean to suggest that you should never accept a trade that provides you with an advantage so long as the other party has a clear understanding of what they are getting and finds the trade to be satisfactory. But I think your bartering mantra should be to focus on making fair trades and if you occasionally end up trading up, well that's just a return on your good karma.

4. Bartering isn't just for Trading "Stuff"

Although much of the focus around bartering is on trading goods, you can also barter for services and if you are working on building the skills on the skill-building list, you will have a lot of new skills to offer in trade. Since bartering for skills will be just as important as bartering for stuff in a post-collapse world, I urge you to practice doing that as well.

5. Practice Safe Bartering

In some ways, I look at bartering with a new trading partner the same way I look at blind dating – my personal security has to be the most important thing. This means that you should not be arranging to meet potential bartering partners that you found on the internet at your home or in a private or secluded area. Arrange for initial meetings to be in public places where the proximity of other people helps guarantee your safety.

If the item you are trading is too big to be transported to a neutral location, arrange to meet the potential trade partner somewhere neutral first and then have them follow you to the location of the item rather than providing an address or directions. Never meet with someone at your home alone, always make sure there is someone else there with you.

These same safety guidelines will become even more important in a post-collapse world. When you are trading with new people, never bring the items you are trading to the first meeting and never meet with anyone alone. Do all trading in public and always have enough of your own people present to provide a sense of security. Never trade near where you live and never let new trading partners know where you are living. Practice being safe and cautious now so that it is second nature when the world falls apart.

In addition to those items listed above on the stockpile list, here are some other things you may want to stock up on with the express purpose of using them to barter with.

- Disposable razors and razor blades
- Spices

- Alcohol and wine
- Toothpaste
- Shampoo
- Condoms
- Instant Coffee
- Duct Tape
- Aluminum foil
- Needles
- Thread
- Fishing line

Conclusion

The threat of economic collapse is real and growing every day. The complexity and interconnected nature of the global economy means any economic catastrophe will send ripples around the world. For families, it can be challenging to prep for this kind of threat because there are so many possibilities, variables, and factors at play.

And that is why I wrote this guide. So much of the information available about prepping for economic collapse focuses on anti-government sentiment, purchasing precious metals, and stockpiling supplies without diving into the complex issue of what might cause this kind of catastrophe. But how can you prepare for something if you don't understand the real ramifications and how different economic conditions can impact your family?

After reading this guide, you now have a basic understanding of:
- Why economic collapse is difficult to define
- The common causes of economic collapse
- What each of these possible causes means for you and your family from a preparedness perspective
- The five stages of economic collapse
- What you can expect at each of those five stages
- What economic assets you will need to have at each stage to survive and thrive
- What you can do now to be ready for any economic storm that comes our way

From explaining what the difference between hyperinflation and deflation to outlining what happens when the government can't borrow more money, you now have the basic information you need to understand the different aspects of an economic collapse. You now have actionable steps to help you strengthen your family's position now so that you are ready to withstand a variety of economic conditions. You have the information you need to start assembling the skills and stockpiling the supplies you will need to safeguard your family's future even if the economy turns upside down.

Happy Prepping!

Macenzie

Check out these other
Survival Family Basics Titles...

http://www.amazon.com/dp/B00HG7Y4YS

http://www.amazon.com/dp/B00HYQ55W6

http://www.amazon.com/dp/B00I90UPSK

http://www.amazon.com/dp/B00J1V939S

http://www.amazon.com/dp/B00JXU7OBG

http://www.amazon.com/dp/B00K00DMQE

www.ingramcontent.com/pod-product-compliance
Lightning Source LLC
Chambersburg PA
CBHW071549170526
45166CB00004B/1597